PARDON ME,
MR. PRESIDENT!

'NEXT!'

Newsweek, October 14, 1974

(LURIE'S WEEKLY PAGE IN NEWSWEEK INTERNATIONAL)

PARDON ME, MR. PRESIDENT!

Ranan R. Lurie

Foreword by HARRY REASONER

Quadrangle/The New York Times Book Co.

To Rod, Barry and Daphne
—my tough editors
Love,
Dad

Library of Congress Catalog Card Number: 74-77942

International Standard Book Number: 0-8129-6255-9

CONTENTS

1-31-74

© 1973 The New York Times, SPECIAL FEATURES Syndicate

RANAN LURIE

PRESIDENT GERALD FORD

June 3, 1974

Mr. Ranan R. Lurie
Baldwin Farms North
Greenwich, Connecticut 06830

Dear Mr. Lurie,

Many thanks for your recent note and the caricature.
Is it captioned something like, "On Your Mark....?"

I'm quite certain you know that I did not participate
in track events. If you were thinking of my football,
you forgot the helmet--which I did wear!

Seriously, Mr. Lurie, I appreciate your courtesy and
thoughtfulness. The caricature will now become a
part of the memorabilia of this exciting time in my
life.

With kind regards.

Sincerely,

Gerald R. Ford

GRF:dkc

7

FOREWORD

by Harry Reasoner

I keep at hand a ready file of responses to the contention that there are many things television cannot do that the print medium can do; I am, for obvious reasons, a strong partisan of television journalism. But there is at least one thing newspapers can do that we can't: they can publish the work of perceptive and distinctive editorial cartoonists like Ranan Lurie. The political cartoon is a highly useful form of journalism. I don't know *why* we haven't been able to figure out how to make the screen perform the function of the page in reproducing cartoons—we know enough about animation and simplification and most TV sets are in better condition to reproduce line drawings than they were ten or fifteen years ago—but we haven't. Someone—maybe Lurie—will find a way to do it someday, but in the meantime it is our loss.

The editorial cartoon as the masters draw it—and Ranan is a master —does a number of things. It puts a strong point drawn from complex information into a few simple lines. It has the great artistic function of making a reader suddenly see familiar facts with a new eye. And it has a marvelous factor of continuity when you see the work of the same cartoonist over a period of time; his abstracted and emphasized likenesses become in a way more real than photographs. And the cartoon has another strange virtue and power: in the hands of a Lurie it can be deeply biting, chillingly candid, somehow without being personally offensive. Some of the things Ranan Lurie said about Lyndon Johnson and Richard Nixon, translated clumsily to prose, would have made those men enemies of the writer for life. How do they react to Lurie? They write and ask if they can have the originals for their collections.

Part of this ability to speak strongly without arousing personal resentment lies in the nature of the cartoonist, I suppose. Ranan Lurie has seen a great deal of anger and hatred in his life and he has strong feelings and perceptions about people and policies. But, knowing him, you never sense in him a personal hatred for anyone. He seems to love the people he draws even when he is constrained to paint them as ludicrous or venal or incompetent, and maybe that's the secret of the wide appeal of his cartoons. He is a sophisticated veteran of war and travel and politics, but there is an irrepressible naive delight in him as he looks at good old ridiculous life and good old ridiculous man. We are all the beneficiaries of this combination of perception, talent, energy, and love.

Harry Reasoner

WHAT WORLD LEADERS

"I always admire the sagacity and wit of great caricaturists and I find these qualities so abundantly evident in this latest book of yours. Many warm thanks for this enrichment to my personal library."

PIERRE TRUDEAU,
Prime Minister of Canada

"It says much for your skill that you were able to catch such detail, such nuances, such delicate facial shadings after so short an acquaintance with me."

E. C. WHITLAM,
Prime Minister of Australia

"You have successfully depicted the distinguishing characteristics of your subjects. As for my cartoon, I cannot say that I have been treated badly. Some recent photos of me will be sent to you shortly. . . ."

ARCHBISHOP MAKARIOS,
former President of the
Republic of Cyprus

"My thanks for sending me your famous 'opinions,' such a colorful and lively addition to my library—and welcome change from my customary reading material—is most appreciated."

HENRY A. KISSINGER

SAY ABOUT HIS CARTOONS

"Your talent and political insight are most evident, and I commend you on your continually fresh approach to the issues of the day. Clearly, a cartoonist's pen provides journalism's quickest critique of how those of us in government are—or are not—performing our tasks. I hope my future actions will allow you to utilize them [his photographs—Quadrangle] with your normal and reasonable mixture of candor and kindness."

JAMES SCHLESINGER,
Secretary of Defense

"The pungent eloquence of your cartoons reminded me of the Japanese proverb, 'Eyes are as eloquent as lips.' I was most interested to see how these cartoons, with hardly any verbal captions, managed to convey effectively a number of messages, some of which, as you may be aware, I did not share readily."

MASAYOSHI OHIRA,
Japan's Minister of Foreign Affairs

"A cartoonist has a freedom and sense of fun which people in public life can only envy. I experienced some of it while looking at the contents of your latest book. It was by no means impaired when I saw my own caricature in it."

ZULFIKAR ALI BHUTTO,
Prime Minister of Pakistan

"Excellent and perceptive drawings . . ."

KURT WALDHEIM,
Secretary General of the U.N.

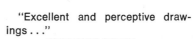

11

"[Your book] will be a treasured addition to my library, and I look forward to finding a moment or two, from time to time, to lighten my official preoccupations by the smiles that your far-ranging and revelatory talent can elicit."

ABBA EBAN,
Minister for Foreign Affairs, Israel

". . . As a former *Lampoon* cartoonist myself, I can all the more appreciate the really keen perception of your work. And now that I think about it, the personalities who came to such prominence the past year provided you with a great source of caricatural characters. . . . I shall look forward to future editions."

ELLIOT L. RICHARDSON

"Your new book, *Nixon Rated Cartoons*, is superb. . . . You are a gifted man."

GEORGE McGOVERN,
Senator

"*Nixon Rated Cartoons* is great. . . ."

MELVIN R. LAIRD

12

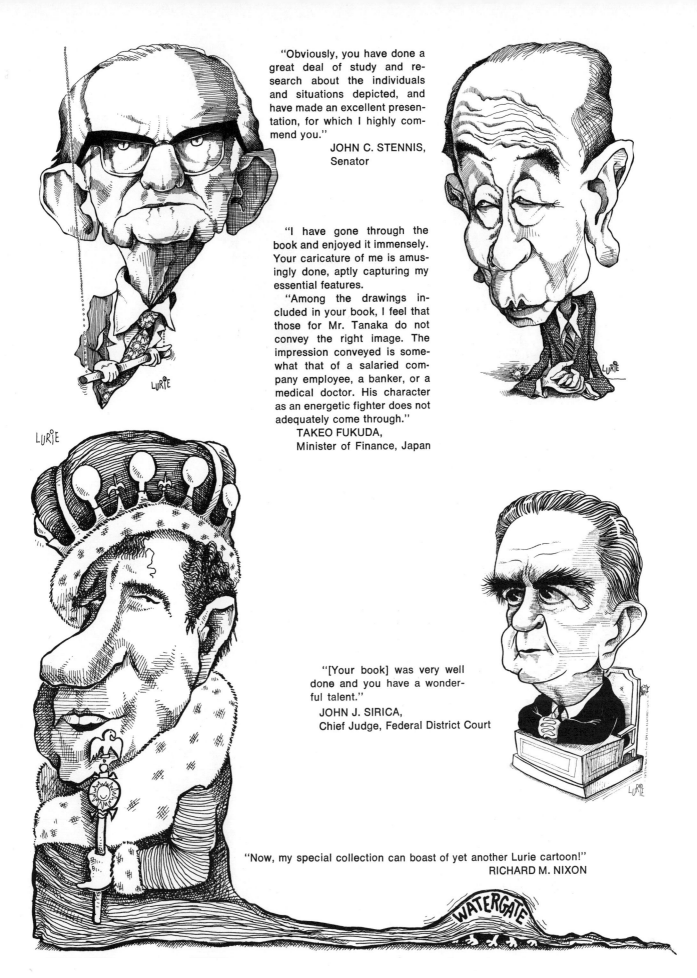

"Obviously, you have done a great deal of study and research about the individuals and situations depicted, and have made an excellent presentation, for which I highly commend you."

JOHN C. STENNIS,
Senator

"I have gone through the book and enjoyed it immensely. Your caricature of me is amusingly done, aptly capturing my essential features.

"Among the drawings included in your book, I feel that those for Mr. Tanaka do not convey the right image. The impression conveyed is somewhat that of a salaried company employee, a banker, or a medical doctor. His character as an energetic fighter does not adequately come through."

TAKEO FUKUDA,
Minister of Finance, Japan

"[Your book] was very well done and you have a wonderful talent."

JOHN J. SIRICA,
Chief Judge, Federal District Court

"Now, my special collection can boast of yet another Lurie cartoon!"
RICHARD M. NIXON

WATERGATE

"About your book . . . please do more. With the humility of the politician, I will keep looking for myself in your forthcoming works of art."

HENRY M. JACKSON,
Senator

"Dear Ranan:
You certainly need not worry about this senator's nose and ears. The way they always look in photographs, anything you did to them in caricature would be an improvement. I am looking forward to sitting down with your book for an afternoon's pleasure."

BIRCH BAYH,
Senator

"Thank God for a country that has something called freedom of the press.

"Your caricature of Scali has shared mixed emotions. My wife and daughters believe it doesn't do justice to the Scali beauty, but I believe it's great."
JOHN SCALI,
U.S. Representative to the U.N.

"I enjoyed it [Nixon Rated Cartoons—Quadrangle] very much for it's filled with good humor—the kind we can use!"
RONALD REAGAN,
Governor

14

"Dear Ranan:
As a U.S. Senator from Connecticut, I take a great pride in you and your tremendous ability."
LOWELL P. WEICKER,
Senator

"I have always envied the ability of a good political cartoonist who can get to the point of an issue with a line or two. . . . Your book is among the best I have seen."
EDMUND S. MUSKIE,
Senator

"Dear Ranan:
Your skill amazes me. It is said that television sees beneath the skin but nowhere nearly as well as does the perceptive cartoonist. Your book is an amusing mirror of our times and of those who shaped them."
HUGH SCOTT,
Republican Leader, U.S. Senate

"Great book. The cartoons are absolutely fantastic. . . . I felt flattered to be included in that book and, as a matter of fact, except for a grumpy comment or two by my wife, secretary, and daughter, the rest of us thought the likeness of me was pretty darn good. My wife said I looked mean and sour, and I said to her that if she'd been Chairman of the National Committee all during the year of Watergate, how would she look."
GEORGE BUSH, Chairman,
Republican National Committee

1974

5

MR. POLITICIAN

11-14-73

by Ranan Lurie

18

12-29-73

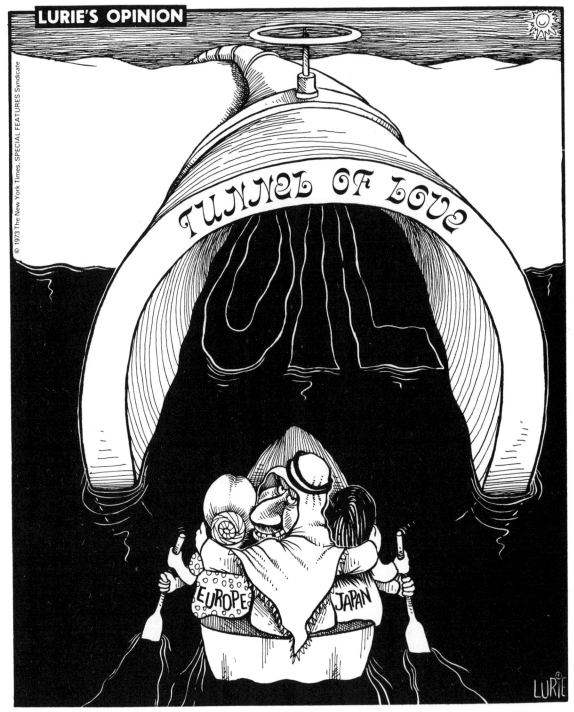

TUNNEL OF LOVE

EUROPE

JAPAN

LURIE

20

12-5-73

by Ranan Lurie

MR. POLITICIAN

12-19-73

1-6-74

LURIE'S OPINION

BRITISH LABOR

by Ranan Lurie

1-5-74

LURIE'S OPINION

MR. POLITICIAN

12-12-73

1-9-74

LURIE'S OPINION

"FINALLY WE TAUGHT HER TO MOVE IN STYLE!"

by Ranan Lurie

1-10-74

ALEXANDER SOLZHENITSYN

MR. POLITICIAN

"OPERATION CANDOR"

"OPERATION CANDOR"

1-8-73

LURIE'S OPINION

MIDDLE EAST

DISENGAGEMENT

26

by Ranan Lurie

1-10-74

LURIE'S OPINION

SOUTH VIETNAM

U.S. TAXPAYERS MONEY

LURIE

1-11-74

29

1-18-74

PRESIDENT SUHARTO OF INDONESIA

RONALD ZIEGLER
PRESIDENT NIXON'S SPOKESMAN

KING BHUMIBOL OF THAILAND

JOHN M. DOAR
DIRECTOR OF SENATE JUDICIARY COMMITTEE STAFF

1-16-74

© 1973 The New York Times, SPECIAL FEATURES/CORES Syndicate

RANAN LURIE

PRESIDENTIAL SIGNATURE

MR. POLITICIAN

© 1973 The New York Times SPECIAL FEATURES Syndicate

MIDDLE EAST NEGOTIATIONS

MIDDLE EAST NEGOTIATIONS

MIDDLE EAST NEGOTIATIONS

1-23-74

1-21-74

LURIE'S OPINION

MILK FUND

ITT AFFAIR

CANDOR

OPERATION

RANAN LURIE IN NEWSWEEK

32

MIDDLE EAST
NEGOTIATIONS

by Ranan Lurie

LURIE'S OPINION

1-22-74

© 1973 The New York Times, SPECIAL FEATURES Syndicate

IMPEACHMENT

1-24-74

© 1973 The New York Times, SPECIAL FEATURES Syndicate

LURIE'S OPINION

NATIONAL ECONOMY

BIG OIL CO. PROFITS

"GULP!"

33

2-6-74

SENATOR HENRY M. JACKSON

"HERE - GO BUY YOURSELF A CUP OF COFFEE"

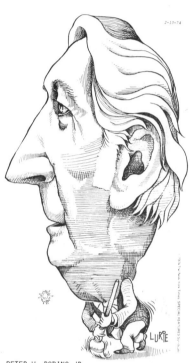

PETER W. RODINO JR.
CHAIRMAN OF THE HOUSE JUDICIARY COMMITTEE

"THE RATIONS ARE COMING! THE RATIONS ARE COMING!"

© 1974 The New York Times, SPECIAL FEATURES Syndicate

RANAN LURIE

© 1974 The New York Times, SPECIAL FEATURES Syndicate

1-29-74

© 1974 The New York Times, SPECIAL FEATURES Syndicate

3-13-74

LURIE'S OPINION

"WHATEVER YOU SAY, SIR!"

MR. POLITICIAN

3-27-74

by Ranan Lurie

"O.K.: NOW I COMMAND YOU TO RETURN TO THE BOTTLE!"

PUTTING THE HEAT ON HEATH

MR. POLITICIAN

4-17-74

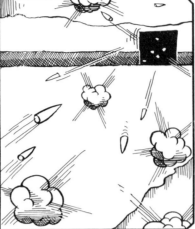

by Ranan Lurie

© 1974 The New York Times, SPECIAL FEATURES Syndicate

GENERAL HUGO BANZER SUAREZ
BOLIVIA'S PRESIDENT

ERIC GAIRY
PRIME MINISTER OF GRENADA

"RELAX, UNCLE - MAYBE THIS TIME I WON'T MISS!"

2-7-74

QUIT!

PUBLIC OPINION

© 1974 The New York Times, SPECIAL FEATURES Syndicate

RANAN LURIE

THE EXORCIST

45

SUEZ CANAL

PANAMA CANAL

HOUSE JUDICIARY COMMITTEE

Executive Privilege

2-13-74

48

"RELAX — I'M GIVING YOU YOUR FAIR SHARE"

"I SAID I'LL PUT YOU BEHIND BARS, SOLZHENITSYN!"

"SO WHAT IF I'VE BECOME AN INTELLECTUAL!"

ADMIRAL THOMAS H. MOORER
CHAIRMAN OF THE JOINT CHIEFS OF STAFF

MICHEL JOBERT
FRENCH FOREIGN MINISTER

ALDO MORO OF ITALY

"REAL OASIS OR FATAMORGANA?"

"YES! FROM NOW ON WE ARE EQUAL!"

51

UP UP AND AWAY!

JEREMY THORPE
BRITISH LIBERAL PARTY LEADER

JOHN T. DUNLOP
COST OF LIVING COUNCIL DIRECTOR

"THIS IS... NEW CAPTAIN... SPEAKING..."

"WOULD YOU INTRODUCE ME TO YOUR PUBLISHERS, AGNEW?"

KING HUSSEIN OF JORDAN

PREMIER PIERRE MESSMER OF FRANCE

THE RAIN DANCER

LURIE IN NEWSWEEK INTERNATIONAL

3-12-74

BRITAIN: STARTING THE BIG DRIVE

3-12-74

"LET'S GET 'EM!"

3-16-74

"I WILL NOT RESIGN... I WILL NOT RESIGN... I WILL NOT RESIGN...."

3-14-74

"WE CAN'T KEEP ON MEETING THIS WAY!"

LURIE'S OPINION

"ET TU, BREZHNEV?"

JAMES ST. CLAIR COUNSEL TO PRESIDENT NIXON

SENATOR CHARLES H. PERCY (R-ILL.)

"I'LL BE DARNED - GRANDMA ELOPED WITH AN ARAB!"

3-21-74

LURIE

"WAIT... I'VE CHANGED MY MIND!"

PREMIER MARCELLO CAETANO OF PORTUGAL

© 1974 The New York Times, SPECIAL FEATURES Syndicate

TALKING TO EACH OTHER, AT LAST

EIRE'S PRIME MINISTER COSGRAVE

LURIE'S OPINION

INCOME TAX LOOPHOLES

"MY NET VALUE IS GONE!!!"

©1974 The New York Times, SPECIAL FEATURES Syndicate

NUCLEAR ARMS TALKS

3-28-74

LURIE'S OPINION

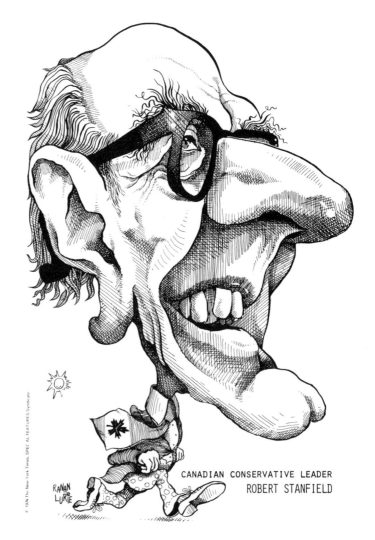

CANADIAN CONSERVATIVE LEADER
ROBERT STANFIELD

AN EQUAL OPPORTUNITY EMPLOYER

MOUTH TO MOUTH RESUSCITATION

PRINCE SOUPHANOUVONG
LEADER OF PATHET LAO FORCES

PREMIER MANEA MANESCU OF RUMANIA

"WELL, HE IS KEEPING HIS PROMISE TO IMPROVE
THE NATION'S ECONOMY."

ENERGY CRISIS

HENRY KISSINGER

© 1974 The New York Times, SPECIAL FEATURES Syndicate   4-14-74

RANAN LURIE

WEST EAST

4-12-74

ELECTIONS '74

HANDICAPPED

"AND I THOUGHT HE WAS A PAPER UNCLE!"

4-16-74

© 1974 The New York Times, SPECIAL FEATURES Syndicate.

"WOMEN AND CHILDREN FIRST!"

LURIE'S OPINION

MID-EAST

U.N.

SENATOR EDWARD KENNEDY (D-MASS)

4-13-74

WILLIAM SIMON

OPERATION CINDERELLA

4-19-74

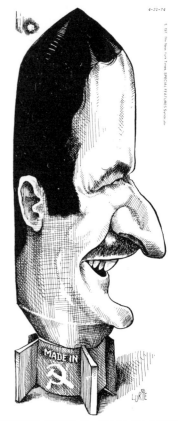

PRESIDENT HAFEZ-AL-ASSAD OF SYRIA

JACQUES CHABAN-DELMAS OF FRANCE

"GIDDI-HUP "

LURIE'S OPINION

"CAN'T HEAR YOU!"

"HERE, NOW YOU'LL FEEL MORE COMFORTABLE"

FRANÇOIS MITTERRAND OF FRANCE

YITZHAK RABIN,
PRIME MINISTER DESIGNATE OF ISRAEL

"WHEN WILL WE ARRIVE, HARRY?"

GENERAL ANTONIO DE SPINOLA
NEW RULER OF PORTUGAL

VALÉRY GISCARD D'ESTAING OF FRANCE

5-15-74
MR. POLITICIAN
G.O.P.
SUPPORT
MY CAREER
PORT
MY TRANSCRIPT
MY CAREER
MY CAREER
© 1974 The New York Times, SPECIAL FEATURES Syndicate
by Ranan Lurie©

4-30-74
LURIE'S OPINION
MID-EAST
©1974 The New York Times, SPECIAL FEATURES Syndicate
LURIE©

"MY FEET ARE KILLING ME!"

4-29-74

RANAN LURIE
THE PHILADELPHIA BULLETIN

"LIGHT AT THE END OF THE TUNNEL!"

"I FANCY THE HARD STUFF, LIKE TAPES..."

"WOULD YOU BUY A USED ENCYCLOPAEDIA FROM THIS MAN?"

ENERGY PRINCE JOHN SAWHILL

"NO MORE PRESIDENTIAL LANGUAGE IN THIS HOUSE, SON!"

LURIE'S OPINION

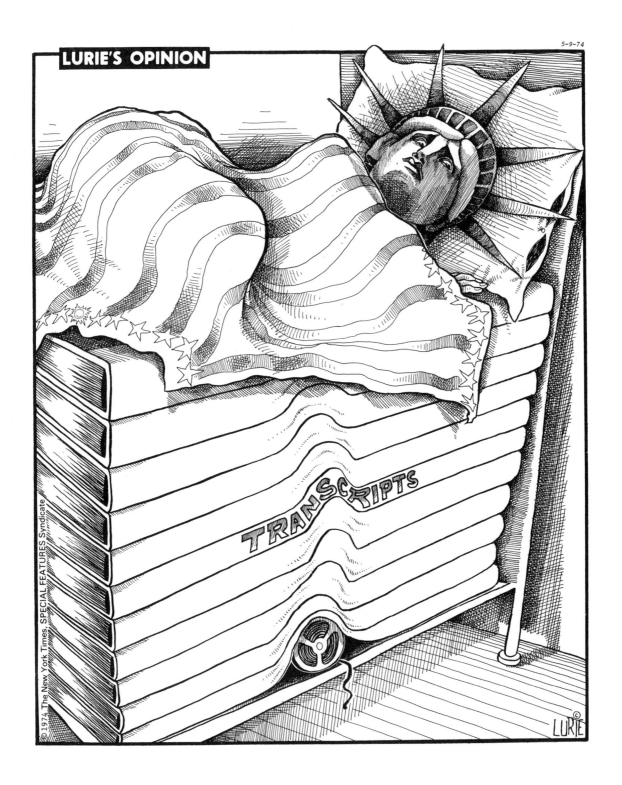

TRANSCRIPTS

LURIE

5-8-74

5-9-74

DIGNITY

BRANDT

© 1974 The New York Times, SPECIAL FEATURES Syndicate

LURIE

© 1974 The New York Times, SPECIAL FEATURES Syndicate

5-11-74

READY FOR CORONATION

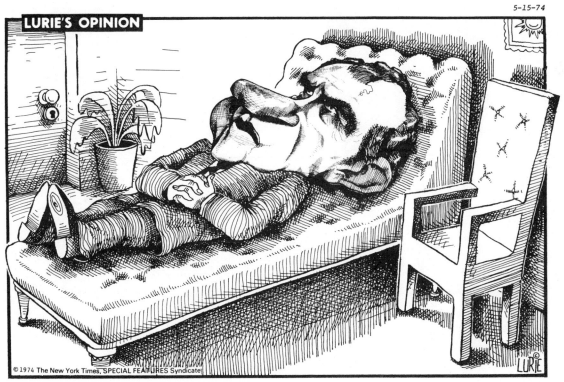

"DOCTOR... NO ONE WANTS TO LISTEN TO ME ANYMORE."

LURIE'S OPINION

"HOLY MOSES - IT MIGHT WORK!"

5-29-74

5-24-74

"FOR THE LAST TIME - WILL YOU COME OUT?!"

5-24-74

LEON JAWORSKI, WATERGATE SPECIAL PROSECUTOR

5-25-74

WALTER SCHEEL, WEST GERMANY'S PRESIDENT

GERMANY'S FOREIGN MINISTER, HANS-DIETRICH GENSCHER

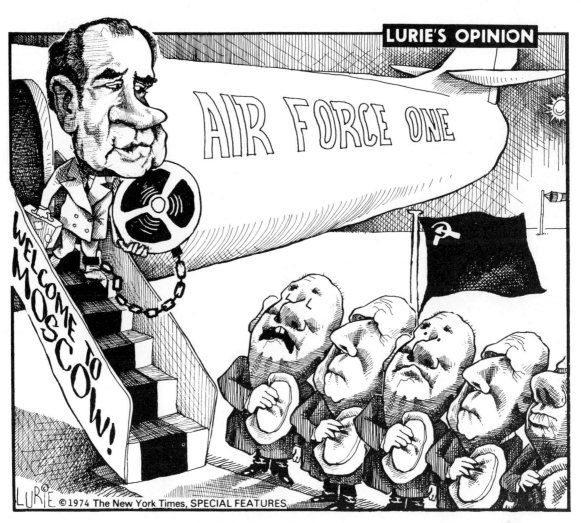

5-26-74   "COMRADES - THE PRESIDENT OF THE UNITED STATES!"

WHITE HOUSE LAWYER J. FRED BUZHARDT JR.

EDWARD HUTCHINSON
HOUSE JUDICIARY COMMITTEE

LURIE'S OPINION

"THE INFLATION IS BEHIND US"

"IT WAS SO NICE NEGOTIATING WITH YOU, ASSAD"

LURIE'S OPINION

THE WINNER

INDIRA GANDHI, PRIME MINISTER OF INDIA

KENNETH RUSH,
CHIEF ECONOMIC COORDINATOR

SUBPOENA CONCERTO

"WILL THE REAL GERALD FORD PLEASE STAND UP?!"

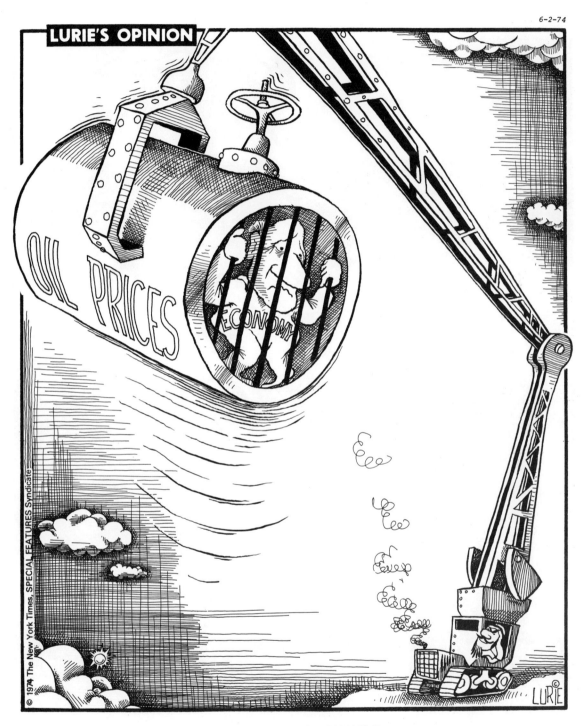

"UP UP AND AWAY!"

LURIE'S OPINION

MID-EAST

SCANDALS

SCANDALS

HENRY

© 1974 The New York Times SPECIAL FEATURES Syndicate

LURIE

LURIE'S OPINION

MIDDLE

EAST

LURIE

6-7-74

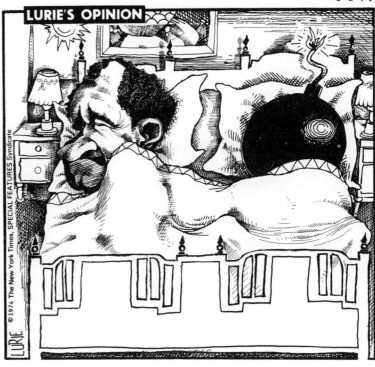

"ARE YOU STILL THERE, COLSON?"

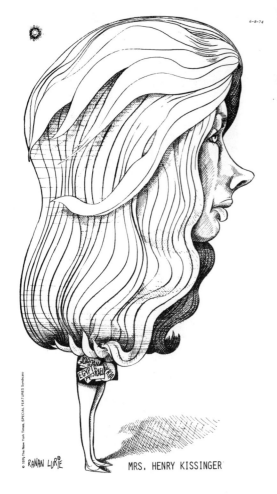

MRS. HENRY KISSINGER

CHARLES W. COLSON, PRESIDENT NIXON'S FORMER AIDE

"THE TENANT IS PROBABLY ABROAD"

HELMUT SCHMIDT,
GERMANY'S CHANCELLOR DESIGNATE

GENERAL ASSAD,
PRESIDENT OF SYRIA

"MOUNT RUSHMORE IT AIN'T, BUT..."

WIRETRAPPED

SHOWING THEIR TEETH

"PEACE!"

ITALY'S PRESIDENT GIOVANNI LEONE

JUDGE GERHARD A. GESELL

LURIE'S OPINION

"HELP, AMERICA! I JUST BLEW MY BUDGET!"

LURIE'S OPINION

U.S.A.

LURIE

BACK FROM THE MIDDLE EAST

LURIE'S OPINION

120   6-25-74

6-22-74

LURIE'S OPINION

POPULARITY

INTERNATIONAL SUCCESS

inflation

The New York Times, SPECIAL FEATURES Syndicate

LURIE

121

LURIE'S OPINION

© 1974 The New York Times, SPECIAL FEATURES Syndicate

LURIE

"WOW...THESE RUSSIANS SURE DRIVE A HARD BARGAIN!"

"I ALREADY GAVE IN RUSSIA."

6-29-74

RANAN LURIE

PRESIDENT RICHARD M. NIXON

125

126

FOURTH OF JULY 1974

"YOU'RE S U R E YOU HAVE NOTHING ELSE TO DECLARE?!"

LURIE'S OPINION

7-3-74

DÉTENTE

yalta
weapons
pact

© 1974 The New York Times SPECIAL FEATURES Syndicate

7-2-74

MARIA ESTELA MARTINEZ DE PERON
ACTING PRESIDENT OF ARGENTINA

6-21-74

SENATOR JOHN J. SPARKMAN

129

7-10-74

"I'M AFRAID WE'RE TOO LATE"

7-12-74

CLARENCE M. KELLEY, F.B.I. DIRECTOR

7-3-74

130

7-5-74

THE GREAT BALANCING SHOW

7-11-74

7-14-74

CHIEF JUSTICE WARREN BURGER

7-14-74

"FIRE!"

FRANCINE IRVING NEFF
NEW U.S. TREASURER

7-13-74

HOW WILL THEY USE THE GAVEL?

7-31-74

by Ranan Lurie

133

LURIE'S OPINION

EARTHQUAKE

COLONEL VASCO DOS SANTOS GONCALVES
NEW PREMIER OF PORTUGAL

NIKOS GIORGIADES SAMPSON NEW CYPRUS BOSS

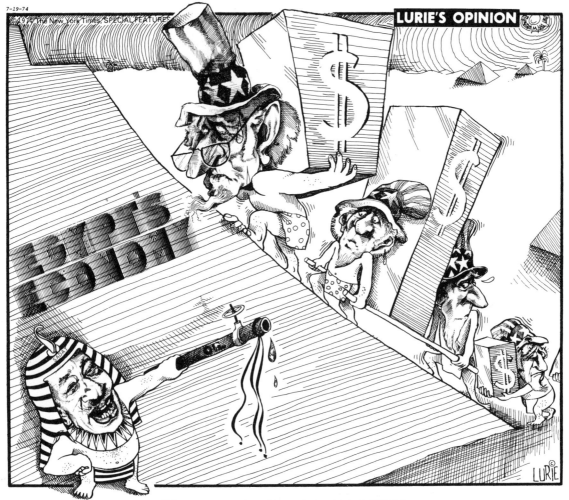

"JUST LIKE IN THE GOOD OLD DAYS!"

MR. POLITICIAN

by Ranan Lurie

7-20-74

© 1974 The New York Times, SPECIAL FEATURES Syndicate

DIVERSION TACTICS

7-26-74

CONSTANTINE CARAMANLIS, PREMIER OF GREECE

7-23-74

PREMIER BULENT ECEVIT OF TURKEY

7-26-74

NO ONE IS ABOVE THE LAW

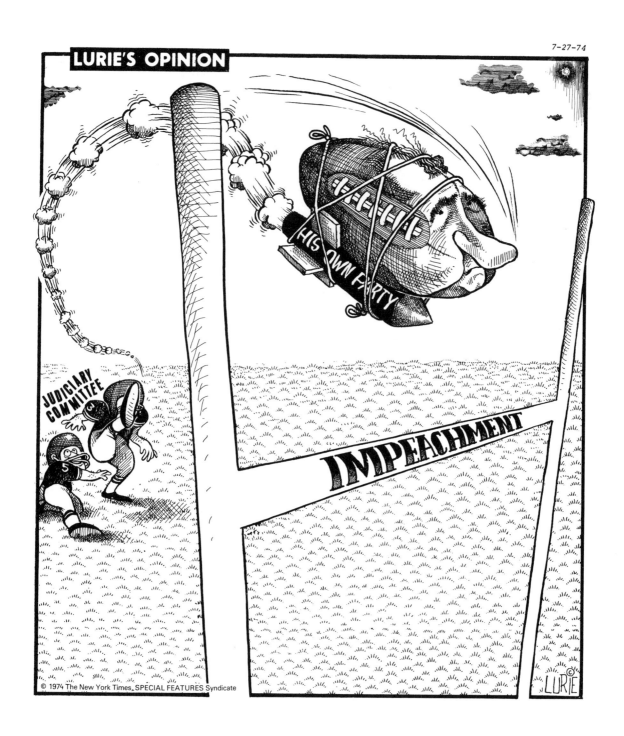

7-29-74

LURIE'S OPINION

SALE!

sale

Bargains

SALE!

50% OFF!!!

THE SHAH

© 1974 The New York Times, SPECIAL FEATURES Syndicate

LURIE

8-3-74

PRESIDENT CHUNG HEE PARK OF SOUTH KOREA

LURIE IN NEWSWEEK INTERNATIONAL

7-25-74

PRINCE JUAN CARLOS DE BORBÓN OF SPAIN

© 1974 The New York Times, SPECIAL FEATURES Syndicate

LURIE

141

7-30-74

142

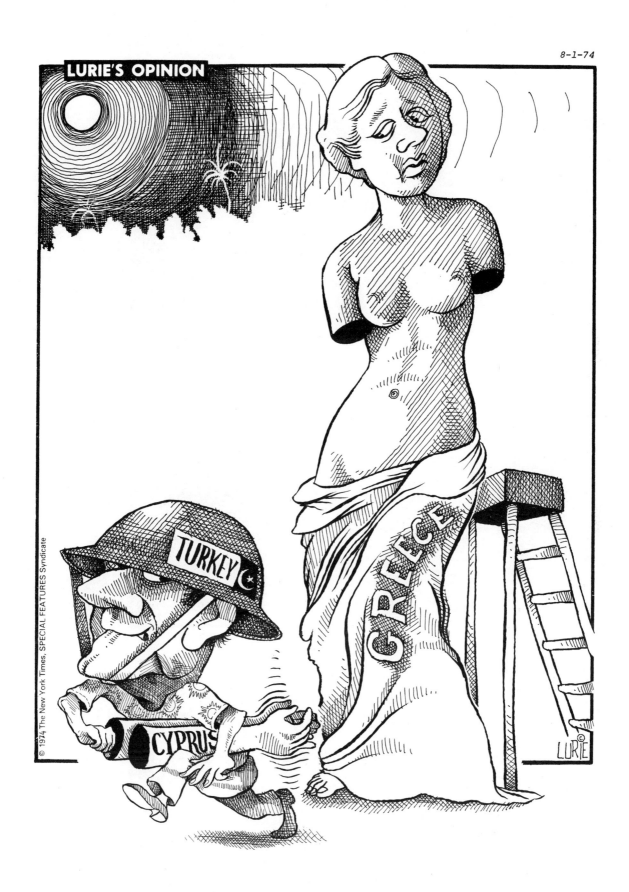

LURIE'S OPINION

© 1974 The New York Times, SPECIAL FEATURES Syndicate

TURKEY

CYPRUS

GREECE

LURIE

"PERHAPS WE SHOULD CHANGE OUR STRATEGY, MR. PRESIDENT"

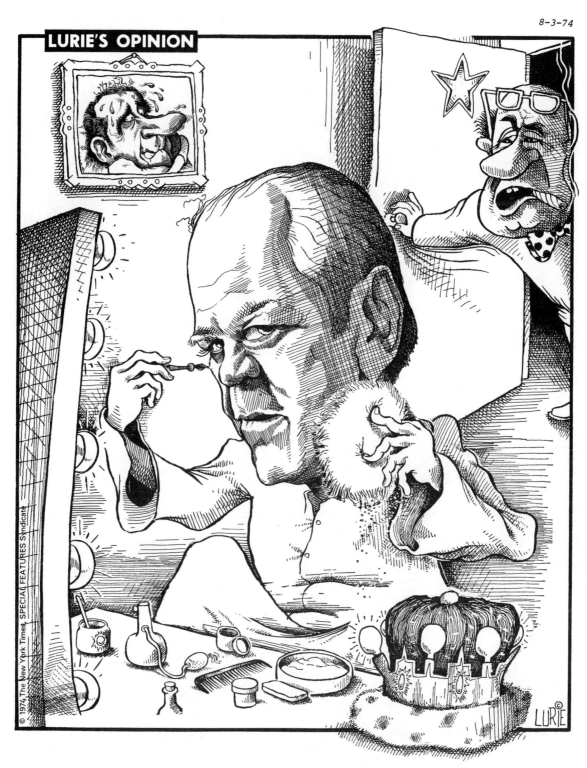

"BETTER HURRY!"

8-3-74

MR. POLITICIAN

8-6-74

HOSTAGE

8-7-74

by Ranan Lurie

8-7-74

"P L E A S E, CHILDREN..."

8-8-74

8-9-74

LURIE

8-12-74

MR. POLITICIAN

8-14-74

8-16-74

THE UNEMPLOYED

by Ranan Lurie

© 1974 The New York Times, SPECIAL FEATURES Syndicate

9-1-74

© 1974 The New York Times, SPECIAL FEATURES Syndicate

CYPRIOT PRESIDENT GLAFCOS CLERIDES

155

8-15-74

LURIE'S OPINION

GREECE

Turkey

CYPRUS

PEACE TALKS

© 1974 The New York Times, SPECIAL FEATURES Syndicate

LURIE

156

SPAIN

LURIE

GENERALISSIMO FRANCISCO FRANCO, RULER OF SPAIN

8-18-74
CONSERVATIVES
LIBERALS
LURIE
The New York Times, SPECIAL FEATURES Syndicate

PRESIDENT GERALD R. FORD

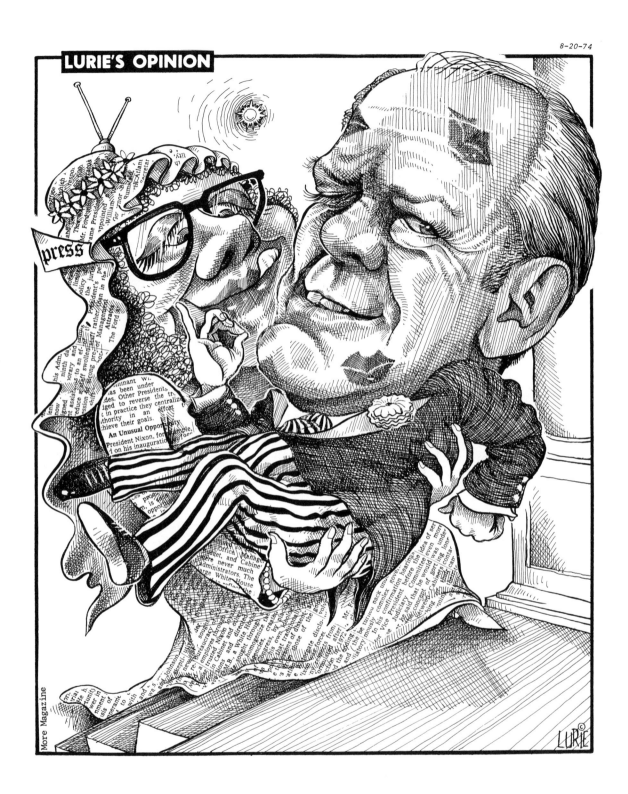

8-20-74

More Magazine

160

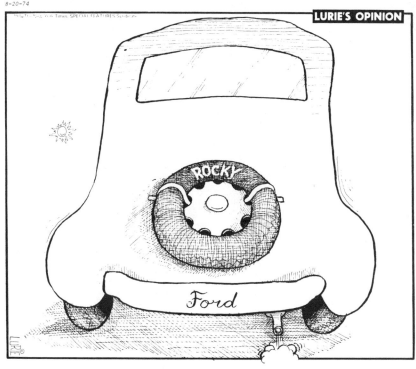

161

"DON'T WORRY, JERRY - IF CONGRESS WON'T APPROVE THE FOREIGN AID BILL, I'LL FEED INDIA"

VICE PRESIDENT DESIGNATE NELSON A. ROCKEFELLER

"NEXT!"

LURIE'S OPINION

"BETTER MOVE BACK, FELLAS..."

8-28-74

MR. POLITICIAN

© 1974, The New York Times, SPECIAL FEATURES Syndicate

by Ranan Lurie

8-27-74

PRIME MINISTER ABDUL RAZAK OF MALAYSIA

"THERE GOES THE NEIGHBORHOOD!"

8-23-74

LURIE

KING CONSTANTINE OF GREECE

LURIE'S OPINION

NEW FEDERAL HOUSING PROPOSALS

LURIE

"LOOKS GREAT FROM HERE!"

"HERE'S THE RANSOM..."

"I FEAR A COLD COLD WINTER AHEAD"

WARNING:
G.O.P. CONSERVATIVES
HAVE DETERMINED THAT
CUBAN CIGAR - SMOKING
IS DANGEROUS TO YOUR
POLITICAL HEALTH!

by Ranan Lurie

9-4-74

WORLD FOOD SHORTAGE

U.S. AID

© 1974 The New York Times, SPECIAL FEATURES.

LURIE

LURIE'S OPINION

DIPLOMATIC BREAKTHROUGH

"CLIMBING BACK WON'T BE AS EASY AS IT WAS SNEAKING DOWN"

9-6-74

LURIE

LUIS CABRAL, GUINEA-BISSAU'S NEW PRESIDENT

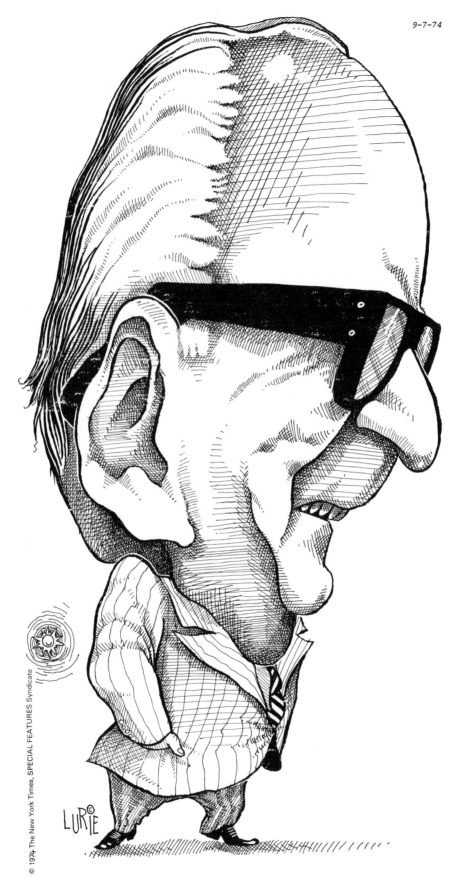

LURIE

MARIANO RUMOR, PREMIER OF ITALY

FIRST DAY IN SCHOOL

9-8-74

"FEEL LIKE STARTING A NEW FORM OF LIFE?"

182

MR. POLITICIAN

"CAST THY BREAD UPON THE WATERGATE...

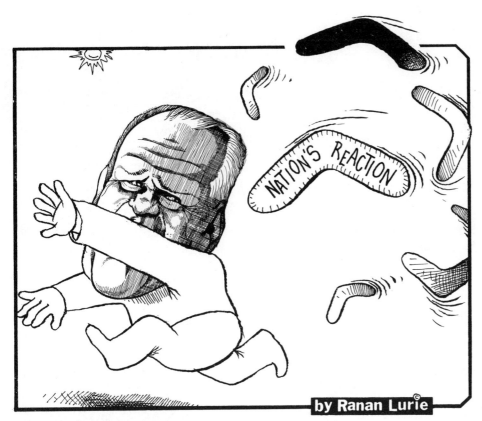

FOR THOU SHALT FIND IT..."

MY POPULARITY

NEW IMPROVED PARDON
BLEACHES WHITEWASHES

LURIE

9-11-74

9-13-74

LURIE'S OPINION

AFRICA

LURIE

LURIE'S OPINION

"PLEASE, PLEASE! THE PRESIDENT HAS ONLY TWO HANDS!"

LURIE

SOUTH AFRICA'S PRIME MINISTER JOHN VORSTER

LURIE

MOZAMBIQUE'S FRELIMO LEADER MACHEL

"WELCOME TO THE MOSCOW MUSEUM OF FINE ARTS!"

193

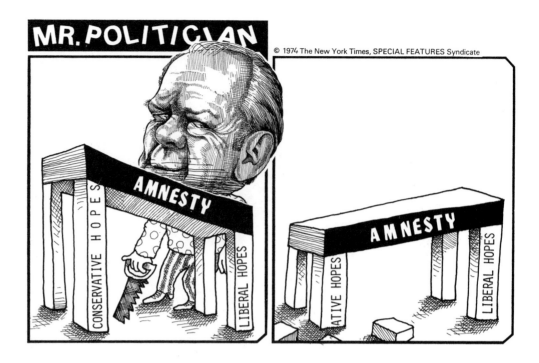

MR. POLITICIAN

AMNESTY

CONSERVATIVE HOPES

LIBERAL HOPES

AMNESTY

ATIVE HOPES

LIBERAL HOPES

9-29-74

LURIE

EDWARD HEATH
BRITISH CONSERVATIVE PARTY LEADER

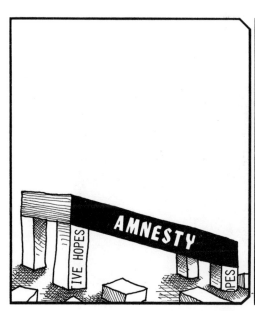

by Ranan Lurie

9-29-74

JEREMY THORPE
BRITISH LIBERAL PARTY LEADER

LURIE

9-19-74

196

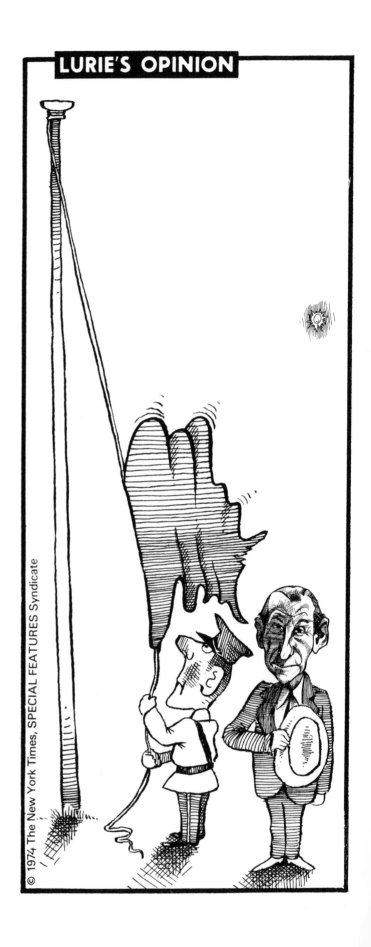

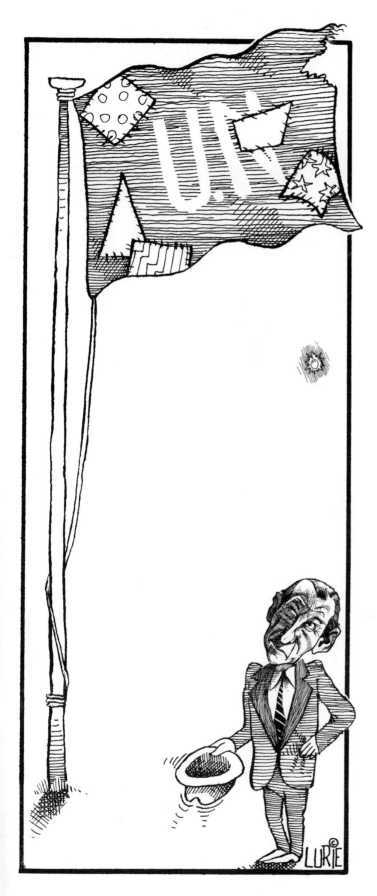

9-20-74

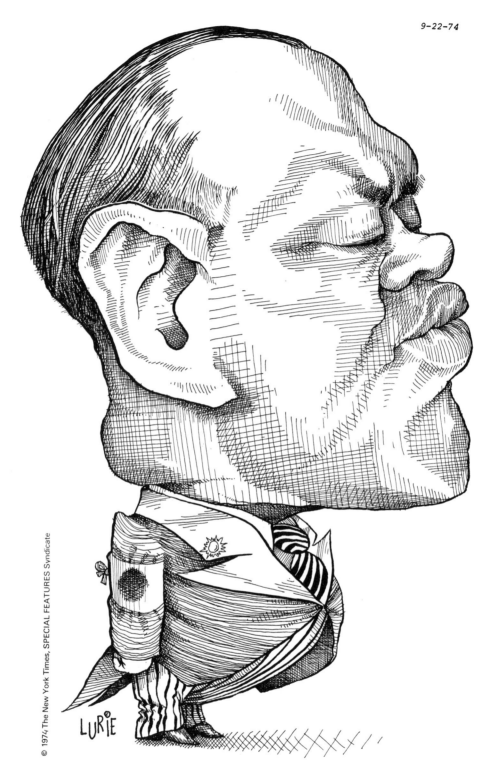

JAPAN'S PRIME MINISTER KAKUEI TANAKA

LURIE'S OPINION

© 1974 The New York Times, SPECIAL FEATURES Syndicate

"I SEE THAT CONGRESS APPROVED A VERY SMALL BUDGET THIS YEAR..."

9-25-74

"HEADS, I TAKE OVER!"

"YES, I'M READY FOR MEANINGFUL RELATIONS!"

9-27-74

206

INTOXICATED

CASTRO

LURIE'S OPINION

OIL EXPENDITURES

© 1974 The New York Times, SPECIAL FEATURES Syndicate

10-19-74

ALAN GREENSPAN
CHAIRMAN OF THE COUNCIL OF ECONOMIC ADVISERS

© 1974 The New York Times, SPECIAL FEATURES Syndicate

LURIE'S OPINION

WESTERN ECONOMIC SUMMIT

© 1974 The New York Times, SPECIAL FEATURES Syndicate

10-1-74

CALIFORNIA GOVERNOR RONALD REAGAN

LURIE

SENATOR LOWELL WEICKER (R-CONN.)

"MY SALARY IS LOUSY... THANK GOODNESS FOR THE TIPS!"

ON THE ROCKY TRAIL

10-22-74

BRITISH PRIME MINISTER HAROLD WILSON

© 1974 The New York Times, SPECIAL FEATURES Syndicate

CONGRESSMAN WILBUR MILLS
CHAIRMAN OF THE WAYS AND MEANS COMMITTEE

10-23-74

MR. POLITICIAN

© 1974 The New York Times, SPECIAL FEATURES Syndicate

10-9-74

by Ranan Lurie

10-7-74

LURIE'S OPINION

© 1974 The New York Times, SPECIAL FEATURES Syndicate

"SHE LOVES ME... SHE LOVES ME NOT..."

218

10-17-74

10-8-74

JACQUES CHIRAC, PREMIER OF FRANCE

10-18-74

STRIPTEASE

"LET'S DRINK TO A LONG POLITICAL LIFE!"

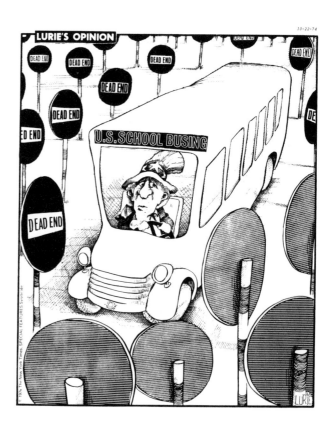

10-23-74

by Ranan Lurie

"ENJOY YOURSELVES, CHILDREN - THESE ARE THE BEST YEARS OF YOUR LIVES!.."

"O.K. - WHERE'S THE ENGINE?!"

PRESIDENT GERALD FORD